scroll,
normal

apocalypse scroll like it was normal

kenji kinz

First published 2021
by Subbed In
www.subbed.in

© kenji kinz 2021

Cover artwork by Trish Phoenix
Book design by Dan Hogan
Text set in 8pt Domaine Text

First edition

Printed and bound in Birraranga (Melbourne)

National Library of Australia Cataloguing-in-Publication:
kinz, kenji
apocalypse scroll like it was normal / kenji kinz
ISBN: 978-0-6451524-0-1 (paperback)

Subbed In 013

All rights reserved.

This book is copyright. Apart from any fair dealing for the purposes of research, criticism, study, review or otherwise permitted under the Copyright Act, no part of this book may be reproduced by any process without permission. Inquiries should be addressed to Subbed In: hello@subbed.in

These sentences were written and published on Dharug, Gadigal, Bidjigal, Gomeroi, Bunurong Boon Wurrung and Wurundjeri Woi Wurrung Land that remains stolen and unsettled. The true custodians of this Land have never ceded their Sovereignty. They and countless others who strive to follow them, in the past and present, fight and survive to maintain the ongoing omnipresence of Indigenous Sovereignty on and of this Country. To inherit that decolonial horizon to pass it on, to maintain and elaborate a hope before and beyond hope, exceeding the here-and-now, refusing 'freedom' because it never asked to be named. This hopes only to be an elaboration of this mutual debt of the undercommons that we share and study together, belonging to everybody, and no one.

Always Was Always Will Be

contents

((noun.) 'things contained' in something (a stomach, a document, etc), from early 15c. Latin continere 'to hold together, enclose', from com 'with, together' + tenere 'to hold' (from root *ten- 'to stretch'))

9   untitled 1 (track 1 [fantasticity])

10   imagine there's a
hole in my leg and
it's bleeding
the same colour
as yours

14   Special Consideration //
Snotty Sheets

18   //S,T,I.L,L/O,N/
D,ЯE.ΔM/L,I,N,E,

20   depressed media student (i am warm under the sun because all data is relational)

22   Whiteness consumes everything without considering long term con sequences. From land to resources to humans. Friendships and relation ships. Memory and affect. Move on because life is transient and fungible. Flesh of my flesh, blood of my blood. In the imperial mind, life begins and ends with possession absolutely and redemption via Christ(/Capital) is guaranteed. For ever and ever, Amen!

28	untitled 2 (track 2 [matters])
31	Little Amigos
34	(Anti)Black World
42	untitled 3
43	dorito mountain
44	Can U Read This? Volume ON Comments OFF
46	untitled 4 (track 3 [suburbidity])
47	'liberty or death!'
49	(Un)Settling
57	weird poem death
61	untitled 5 (track 4 [held])
64	seen
65	we look after each other to remember what came before/ to look after, to see what remains, to feel (in) the wake
67	Reading List
72	One Extra Large Coffin For My Luxury SUV Please
75	untitled 6

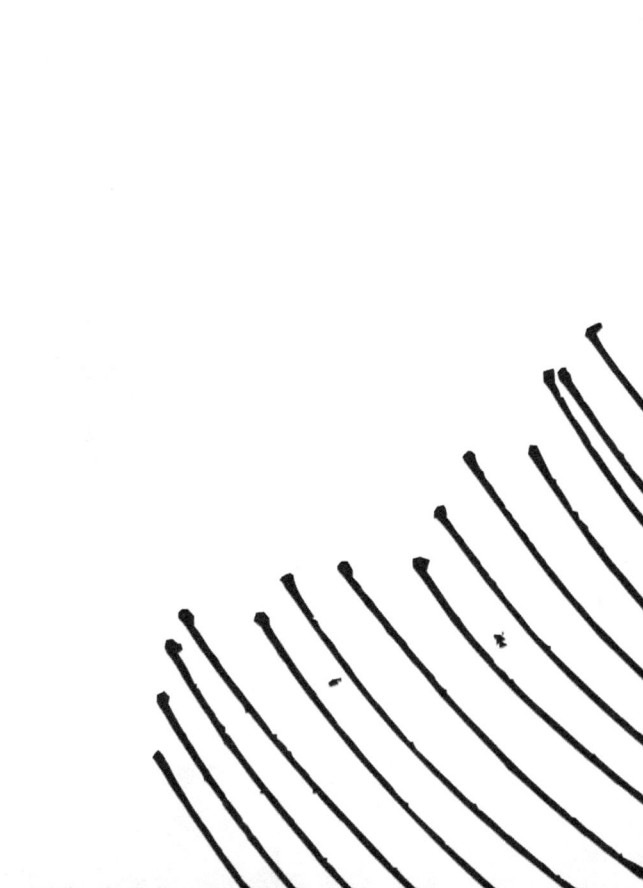

city on lockdown so we stayed on

seen patrolling out there too, too heavy for heaven

something like a bad stink, it sticks to the clothing

carried around like a bad habit, bad news on a bad day

but still, something like an embrace when it all breaks

something euphoric about finally seeing it all fall

you know

something like a phenomenon and that's fantastic

sorta hard to keep a hold of, all worries and wounds

and sorry for all the words, not a lot of sorrow in it

caught in some other (im)possibility of escape

we keep on to follow the pain to find another way

maybe a plan, or maybe just a bit of time to stay here, and play

so sometimes we really don't know

so don't go

city on lockdown so we stayed on

imagine there's a hole in my leg and it's bleeding the same colour as yours

feel the subtle hum of another slow roll down
the great western

slow only because somehow we're still here, arrived
finally like we had never left
holding these moments together with an
unsettling kind of
steadiness
and hefs on the stereo still yelling no effect

but imagine this really
is a rupture and something we don't
recognise really does come pouring out
like we always really knew

it's not hard to imagine, is it?

our life is short, seizing echoes of an unfamiliar music
and all our favourite songs, which always seem to start
and stop … … … … … … but this sound goes forever

i don't want to die, but if the self is illusory then 'i'
was always already dead, tru?

(and then sometimes, in these moments of proximity
amidst what would otherwise be panic
we know that any one of us dies for all of us
we remind each other of the lie of the self
of this future that was never any one's
and give ourselves to all of us
in irresistible celebration
of our irreducible togetherness)

community and history make us us, is there any other thing?

we move in recognition of our memory and the ongoingness of life, language, lore, love, of the everyday material needs and dreams of our friends and communities — people are hungry so feed them. community, those commons that together make us, these things we do together in common, in general, in public... this life we see has never been only some abstract ideal we vaguely work around and towards and only ever expect to arrive at once the big bad game of capitalism is over. it's not a video game. real life continues with absolutely no regard for what anyone wishes to call it. there is work to be done and it seems a grace enough that we can all do that work.

and what about them other ones

who choose instead to shrink entirely behind illusory nonetheless malevolent devices of force, collectively constrained to their ugly and ill//fitting uni-form — aren't they the ones so feverishly obsessed with us and ours? aren't they the ones so viciously committed to struggling against what appears clearly and forcefully as truth, as love, as sovereignty?

aren't you the one resisting us?

      all of this is to say,
            when we say 'jump',
        they always say,
            know no other way
        than to ask us,
    'how high?'

now, imagine

        what the fuck else we could do!

Special Consideration // Snotty Sheets

The screen is black we wrote all over it it's still black

Outside a thousand mangoes not one of them is green

Five dollar five dollar five dollar the whole lot save
for the Sun
like a reflection of an explosive still
of home, a place we learned to forget

Because poetry didn't mean what we thought it meant
and it probably never will! It's a joke, relax,
we don't need to hear how you feel.

In the waiting room a prayer descends from a far away
television, old Arab in the corner behind a fern
watching sports on a smartphone in the lap, the
children playing with shapes at his feet like
alchemy, a steel spoon coiled in the frame of a
future we didn't need to write home about.

Like what if every time we said something, we really did
lose parts of our insides?

What if when we wrote our names we forgot them,
every time, every word?

And what if every time we stepped outside, the
ground really was lava?

After some time it seems
as if 'what if' was never the question,
as if the seemingly unclear is where we've always
seen it the most clearly.

The doctor says it's illegal
to backdate his notes at which point
the floor becomes carpet and I remember myself and
I can't help thinking of his eyebrows
at which point I couldn't really say anything
other than oh,
okay,
that's fine.

//

Okay the dog is leaking out her nose again, wake up Z the dog's fucked, the floor is covered in shit and I'm sweaty. Okay the dog is fucked so what look at this photo we took. Every time I do it makes me gag, remember when we threw up in the park together because all our friends were evil robots? White cedar is the name we gave to that time where all the worms found their way out into the light, and the house fell down, the entire stupid fucken thing! And every mother fucker got what was always coming. So pick the dog up and put her here on the bed who gives a fuck if she's covered in her own snot at least she's being honest about what's inside of her!

//STILL/ON/ D.RE.AM/LINE//

In the steel cage flying towards the storm, the sky grey terminal

A hundred and fifty suits stare at my crying face

I don't care

Stopped caring when the first gum trees fell, the stream brought down a whole native forest

Then it was an old server yard, now it's where some of the old folk stay and swap stories about the old times

Or just sit and worry about that rusty tomb on the shore, still calling for donations of blood

We got bored of counting our blessings so we went back to counting the days

Mouths full of surrender we fell into the fray

Barely a bag of broken bricks and burnt sesame

Little wonder we sank to the bottom soil and found
ourselves being digested by fungi

Memories of a neon shrine atop an origami staircase,
endless paper cranes folding paper cranes endlessly

That's roughly where the floods started, the
dams gave way and the broadcasters revelled in it

Tangerine farm where the school used to be

A thick sea of plastic seats turning

Yellow

depressed media student (i am warm under the sun because all data is relational)

everything is medium, everything is data
all data is potential
for feeling or transformation
mediation is the constant flow of patterned intensities
transformation is the constant
all data is relational

                                        i am warm under the sun
                            because all data is relational

wanna be more positive
shaved my beard so i can smile again
gotta do what u gotta do
all data is potential for feeling or transformation
if i let my facial hair grow too long, i stop looking in mirrors
i see what they see

google search how to stop seeing what they see

                         i am cold and (never) alone
because all data is relational

concerned parents say something about inner happiness

knowing my worth and so fuck what the rest think

like, yeah, but mum, systematically and historically engrained discrimination won't be beaten by a smile OR WILL IT?!, let's find out

i think to myself half jokingly, smiling at a brick

       i hear yelling and inside i vibrate downwards
       it is like when things hurt in a numbing way
       it is like that because all data is relational and
mediation is the constant flow of patterned intensities
         i don't feel it in a moment
i just stare at the screen or at the food or at the floor
                 i will not be scared
                 i am a big boy now
                 i will not be scared
                 i am a big boy now
                 i will not be scared
                 i am a big boy now
                 i will not be scared
                 i will not be scared

Whiteness consumes everything without considering long term consequences. From land to resources to humans. Friendships and relationships. Memory and affect. Move on because life is transient and fungible. Flesh of my flesh, blood of my blood. In the imperial mind, life begins and ends with possession absolutely and redemption via Christ (/Capital) is guaranteed. Forever and ever, Amen!

(In preschool when we were learning about shapes I thought that nothing was actually two dimensional and that there was no such thing as edges or corners. That if you look closely enough at anything it's all holes and layers. Porous and uneven and malleable. A far less or more interesting title to this poem is '(I'm no good at) Colouring In'. As always, you can choose to remember this however you like.)

So many white radicals wanna decolonise the world, still too scared to start with themselves

Living in a share house talking all smash capitalism, still figuring out how to share a fridge

Let's kill all men and destroy patriarchy, got the brown man looking real angry

Let me have my reactionary poem

I need this breathing space

Like how to write the specific ways white women colonise without being seen as aggressive or aberrant

I've never felt more othered than by those who performed their empathy

At least with bigots you know what you're getting, their hatred is pure and uncomplicated

You're all twisted in guilt and misguidance
Fear and, what?

So you want to separate the art from the politics,
the author from the text

Ah yes, the white fantasy of neutrality

Have fun dealing with the feedback

As if whiteness had ever been anything
other than projected abjection

As if another abstraction of purity would finally
set us all free

As if any of this was ever only skin deep

(Sweet how you dilute the history of hip hop to call it
a brand, sweet how you steal the style and still look so
bland, sweet how you smile when you lie, while knowing
you never had to.)

White girls love a bit of this brown rage

White hands on brown bodies

They love the things we say until we say it to their face

Words are cheap, whatever it cost to get em dressed up

X already said, mother fuckers think it's sweet
until you get your chest messed up

(Brown sugar or brown rice,
brown noise and brown boys
Brown eyes big like brown onions,
Brown leaves burning
in a brown paper bag
burning
burning
burning

you say that like someone owes you something
you wonder why the sky keeps falling in on itself
why the dirt you ate as a kid tastes so funny now
why the laughter sounds so much closer to silence

(when you drop everything to feel the weight of what
we came with, is it lighter than you remembered?)

it's true we grow to come to find another path to follow
much like the last and the next
much like the path we're all on
yet there's a fork in the road
roughly the size of your mothers' sacrifice
the only thing we ever really knew to be true

(when you kneel and quietly thank the silence of
our shared song, what bearing does your heart face?)

dad told me to keep your circles small
mitigate the pain of maintaining all the love you knew
you never really had
this love we know, is always here

so what for that love for the rats that
never seemed to have had any of that
and the ratta-tat-tat of the ones
who really don't fucken matter
cuz, i think we matter, don't we?
and we don't mind ...

so what's your problem?

(maybe you and me were not meant to be here at all
maybe we was something closer to sovereign
maybe we was something closer to real
maybe we was something closer to god
maybe you and me were not meant to be a thing at all)

Little Amigos

Sydney the dead and dying city

Someone please tell me why it cost 6.63 to get here
A quarter of an hour of my labour value as a human
being, so that's not half bad I guess

In every body's eyes is lost joy and it's no one's fault

Loud mobs of shiny corporates with their big bags and
fast paces

They pay our friends to lay their concrete

Put some grass in a box for them to sit in and say
'you're welcome. bye bye now.'

Meanwhile we're all still waiting on an actual apology
followed through with meaningful action

Lungs hurt and I take another drag. I don't even hate
myself so what's the deal?

Diamante encrusted lady on site repeats my name like
it's a foreign object, and I feel like a foreign object

Handsome wog driving the truck, he's an actor for TV adverts but mostly just works in logistics, and next door the playground is called Little Amigos

He said to tell my friends I met the wog from the KFC cricket ad, that they'd know what I was talking about

In the middle of a cold business park on a hot summer's night and of course I'm sweaty

The Westfields looming and large, AC inviting us in to roam

Please leave your trolleys here and your trolls in the next room

That was just a joke cuz I'm getting tired of this poem

Eyes close steadfast, can't bear the scene

A lone scooter collecting runaway cargo

Like everyone just emptied them there and left

Asian smooth face seccies at the loading dock ask us why we're here so handsome KFC cricket wog shows them some pieces of paper, and somewhere a speaker crackles some sound in the shape of what we're all forced to think is the very essence of summer

But in reality is an exciting kind of exhaustion that feels more like the heavy shadow of the Sun

A curtain of crickets and mozzies closing

On the final four beers

Warm and slowly spilling

On the greyest concrete

(Anti)Black World

if we are able at all to talk of 'the world' or 'the world as we (un)know it', then we must recognise that (anti)blackness is the fundamental (dis)organising (il)logic of that world, of this world of western modernity, of settler-coloniality and neoliberal capital gone global. we arrive here via histories (and institutions, machines, extractive and alive legacies, ...) of slavery, dispossession and brutality enacted on some groups of people, deemed black, by other groups of people, deemed white. we also arrive here via time spent watching the news, as anti-black narratives and their many violent manifestations continue to delimit the bounds of civility and subjecthood in the context of what Saidiya Hartman has called 'the afterlives of slavery'.

i am thinking of the ███████████ ███████, of the resurfacing hysteria over '████ ████████' in ████████, of the ████████ ████████ in parliament last week, of the prisons across the continent being filled with mostly Indigenous people and of the ongoing and unexplained deaths in custody of too many, of the continuous theft of Indigenous kids and land and much else, of the absence of accountability as state officers, here and abroad, continue to target, harass and murder black people whose only crime was to exist as black in a world structurally incapable of recognising that as human, as life, as matter that matters.

to talk about these as 'examples' however is to risk framing them as exceptional. from the point of view of whiteness, of settlerhood, coloniality and capital, and therefore from the point of view of the world as we (un)know it, these instances of black suffering and death are not exceptional but the structuring rules. if we are able to speak of a logic to this savagery, then we must recognise it as fundamentally the same logic that mandated the intrusion into the 'New World' and the trans-Atlantic slave trade, that saw black bodies as non-things to accumulate and exchange among white hands, that migrated into this continent throughout the 18th and 19th century and, where there were thriving and complex worlds of people and knowledges and cultures, instead saw emptiness, *terra nullius*, vacant land to be claimed and made productive.

in a bid to justify itself, this depraved illogic finds itself in an unending attempt to frame the people who had been living here for hundreds of thousands of years prior, managing the entire continent via some of the most sophisticated eco-philosophies and technologies that the planet might have ever known, as incapable of anything. indeed it is this logic of possession, reason and mastery that continues to drive so many activists, academics and artists alike. it is, to put it simply, the irrational rationality or rationalised irrationality of whiteness, which only ever comes to know itself via the disavowal and denial of blackness. for the white subject, the white city, the white world to thrive, blackness must be repressed, forgotten, erased.

this might appear totalising in its pessimism only if we accept that 'blackness' or 'whiteness' is simply skin-deep, as the renaissance and enlightenment race scientists believed not so long ago. whiteness instead in this equation, for at least the last 500 years and certainly in the contemporary moment, anchors itself in and finds expression via certain racialised notions of progress and rationality, humanism and liberty, inflected through the lens of the self, the individual, or what Sylvia Wynter has called the project of Man. i hope here only to attempt to follow from what i have learned from writers like Wynter, Hartman, Fred Moten, Stefano Harney, Hortense Spillers, Frank Wilderson, Aria Dean, among others, who talk of blackness, in part, as the condition of possibility for this world, the condition of possibility for white subjectivity and modernity to come to be. blackness must similarly remain contextualised as and in its 'para-ontological distinction from those given (to) a privileged understanding of it'. another way to think through this is with the help of Jared Sexton, who talks of blackness as (the) ante/anti-essentialism.

if we understand whiteness as (co-constitutive of) the white or settler subjectivity, as the law and the police and the university and the medical industrial complex, as all the master structures of governance and order that include but extend far beyond the normative prescriptions of intelligibility we're used to discussing, whether it's bodies and genders, state repression of politically or economically targeted activities and communities, or really any thought or expression when brought face to face with the determining and measuring gaze of the normative... if we understand that whiteness is all of these things, then it seems evident that whiteness, as a system of ordering, is only ever able to know and reproduce itself via an exclusion of that which it deems excessive, insufficient, disordered, formless, broken, black.

remember and recognise, again, that we are living through what Saidiya Hartman has called 'the afterlives of slavery'. those who enforce these master structures maintain a tradition that goes as far back as at least the first slave patrols, and yet it was not so long ago that First Nations people here lived under the paternalistic watch of the 'protection' board, denied wages and dignity while working plantations of cotton, sugarcane or cattle. this is continuous. the enclosure, exclusion and exploitation of Bla(c)k people continues to form the fabric and foundation of the modern 'australian' dream, of the modern world writ large. whiteness is nothing more or less than the ongoing choice to accept and continue in this depraved story of ownership and mastery, to take part in, reify and renew this received rot... and what an effort it is to maintain such a deception, to preserve this plot that pains itself and all to forget.

remember and recognise, again, that refusal is the first right, and that our refusal is co-constitutive of this remembrance and recognition of anotherwise, co-constitutive of our ongoing preservation of the surround, before and beyond the imposition of the normative and its assumed totality. remembering and recognising all this, it seems evident that what at first might appear overwhelming in its totality, this weary world that sometimes feels too woeful to withstand, is really another operation, an incoherent, contingent and shifting assemblage that masks countless sites of contestation and negotiation, innumerable instances of unruly and undeterminable unrest, appearing here or there momentarily perhaps as an indifferent step ahead, leaving governance forever playing catch-up, to call back into order, to capture and fix, name and contain that which it chases in its endless fascination.

      falling into this and maybe we find ourselves where we already were. we all eventually pass into the dirt from where we came, and nothing will ever convince me that that's all there is to it. the land, before and after all, is still here, alive and unsettled, unsettling and excessive and as black as anything. black like the bottom of the ocean and the deepest deep of space, black like the infinity of the cave, the womb, the pupil. god, or the things we come close to meaning when we say that, is everywhere in all of this, so it seems there wasn't ever really a choice other than to continue holding on to a faith that exceeds any of the words we put around it. a choice to remember and recognise, to continue finding and following something we can't ever touch. a commitment to a process that exceeds our extremely limited capabilities to imagine, therefore expanding them endlessly in and with all this ugly excess.

of course, there are always other ways to tell or hear the same story, to listen and elaborate and preserve, other ways to see and know, to survive and live and love, many of which escape containment or definition or any measure. it seems even sometimes when we call ourselves otherwise, when we think ourselves radical, we still remain caught in some grand narrative, unable to untangle ourselves from some assumed history, an alternative stream perhaps a bit to the left, yet derived ultimately from the same source. we are all eventually students of marx, who was a student of hegel, who was a student of kant, who was so terrified of his insides he could never look away.

it seems ultimately, for now at least, whatever that all might come to mean, we are all born into a kind of suffocation, a kind of drowning, but why not try to live a little better in our little time together, why not hold on to these old and true things? i don't think it's zero-sum and maybe it's not even dialectical. we all want a dollar for the drama. we all need a meal and a place to stay and hear another's voice. we all feel something like that, living on the same dirt under the same sky. why waste time pretending to be safe, unscathed, pure and unbothered? how to sooner find our ways back to love, since love is all we ever really have, since love is what got us here at all? how to live through all of this with honour and humility, a bit of warmth and a little laughter... questions we all come to answering, in all our ways and times and spaces.

41

can't keep up with a rolling mountain

i dive underneath to taste the mud

still cool, still fresh

never left us like a bad taste, funky on the inside

rotten phosphorescence cuz wealth tastes worse

me my mind rolling with the punches so don't mind me

stay with the trouble as the moon follows the earth even

when the sky falls

even when the old machines stopped right where they were

mouths wide teeth rusted around overgrown tongues of moss glistening in the rain

was thinking about when r asked the wood where it came from

'who's your fucken aunties cuz?'

can't trust a piece of wood that can't say where it's from

doesn't matter what colour it is

that 7/11 wood burns the same, too quickly, no matter where you get it across the whole damn continent

maybe even the planet

fuck that shit

dorito mountain

i wish there was a mountain of doritos
and then there would be a subreddit, r/doritomountain
many would flock to the mountain of doritos, taking
photos with the appropriate hashtags
'at #doritomountain again #whataview #tookabite
#stoked'

some will travel far yet won't go up close, afraid that
the might of the mountain might strike them down
and others yet will only ever learn of the mountain later
on through the memes

and one day it will thunder and rain and the mountain
will become soggy and disgusting

and all the people that were yet to see the mountain
of doritos will feel confused and disappointed, as if
on christmas eve there was breaking world news that
santa had been killed by space police

and someone will write a think piece criticizing doritos
for their oversight and failure to plan

and someone on the news feed will share the article
and add the caption:

'perfect response to this dorito mountain situation.
grateful for the bravery of our country's heroes.'

Can U Read This? Volume ON Comments OFF

looking at facebook makes me feel anger with unspecified directionality. blink, feel eyeballs wobble, blink back keep reading. it says someone who isn't me is looking at me or something so i say something about how it isn't me. 'Can U Read This? Volume ON Comments OFF!'

why can't i stop writing these stupid internet poems. 30 soon. then the only joke left to tell will be where to bury the body. this one, my one. you can have it once it's there. not mine anymore.

i wrote a poem for the grey ones, big eyes wondering if we're still really eating that. i guess so.

((did you forget how to speak? did you forget that you had a mouth, a heart, etc? i wrote this shit on my gravestone. i wrote this shit on my smartphone. i wrote this shit in my own shit and you still said it wasn't worth shit. so tell me again how there is any thing in or about human beings that is not full of shit, and maybe i'll start to give a shit. in the meantime i will be on the rooftops, screaming this shit.

i will not speak for you. i can not speak
for you. i do not know your language.

really i just want a big farm with the whole fam there.
animals and apricots, rainwater tank big enough to sit
on and see every notable celestial event.))

in other words, poetry is not supposed to change the
world, you fucking idiot! did you really just get here?

lol go on write the poem then,
say what you think is gonna happen and then watch,

listen to the difference, try and make it rhyme maybe
just a little

and don't post it on facebook. try hide ur feelings
behind something a little more worth ur life/time/soul.

((buy this book so i can
pay off debt and eat food with my friends
maybe one day buy my dad a red ferrari.))

On the train we fly fast through the sub-urbans, areas we knew growing up as out west, out towards the dusty blue walls that were there, before and after all, always. Easy to erase the lines we don't like when we don't know the names before ours, when we've forgotten the names before and after names, before the glass walls they built in the middle of everything, on these black hills they painted green, silver, white. How to begin a story with history, a movement with(out) tradition, a song with(in) silence? It's near parramatta, I guess, or something like that, the background chatter mistaken as noise, a broken signal mistaken as an absence of something much more and less than beauty, an absence of something much more and less than living. At the vacant end of the red tiled avenue, in the warm air through the open car park atop towers of plastic prophets, and all the grey gum leaves we threw at each other like confetti, not so long ago— we still felt it, didn't we? So much more than empty, so much in excess of whiteness, even and especially in our loud and unruly disavowals of that emptiness that felt so forcefully material, so materially suffocating, slow, always encroaching. We wanted to run, to fly, of course, but isn't that the point? Not only in transit to some place else but instead as that fugitive move itself, that movement of (im) possibility and our irrepressible memory of it that exceeds us, this unsettled and unsettling celebration of what has always been and always will be. On the screen a funny old face says something 'bout the 'burbs and you blink back to the present, the carriage squeaking through a passage under clouds of light and rain, the infinite blackness of space still there, beyond and before and all around, barely veiled. She clips her nails and speaks another language, and once again you forget your body to remember yourself. We are now targeting antisocial behaviour and fare evasion. You will be fined for placing your feet on the ground.

'liberty or death!'

in the scroll of a home
for us all here way out before the end
of terms, of the moment
look it's still there
round vinegar hill to victoria avenue where the giant grey gums still
drop leaves on the luxury SUVs
on the double lane roundabout to some new civic
infrastructure
a promise, a gift, a sacrifice
to the most committed and steadfast believers
that their time out there on the
new frontier would be
worth all the things
they forgot
to find it

oh a home find us here
where we always were, caught up in some war
at the end of language and greed, where it all runs
into mud, so come down here
fall into this sweet scroll,
this stream of another where maybe
we melted into you
and we won't forget,
we don't want it just all of it, just a moment
of your time, just hungry
cuz we gotta be

(Un)Settling

settlers are foundationally resistant to be(com)ing unsettled/unsettled be(com)ing(s). it could be described as an onto-epistemological resistance, an inher(it)ed (pre)condition, an unthinking yet thinkable kind of malaise. (onto, from the greek ontos, 'being', and episteme, 'knowledge' — in heart and head.)

in other words, settlers are sick and the sickness is settlement, where settlement is a serial straining to contain, name, regulate and rule, an imposed interruption to an already and always existing immanence — of life and living, of spirit and sovereignty.

(thinking sickness slightly differently, settlement is also a serial denial of this dis-ease that drives and delivers us, the broken and beautiful common (under) grounds we share that keep us ill and infectious in the face of an evil, unhealthy kind of wellness.)

consider (the reality) that what's here is what was always here and what will always be here, which means the settler is in fact the one acting in resistance, strained ceaselessly to maintain and elaborate the unreality of settlement. what we often mistake as our resistance is maybe better understood as a recognition, a remembering, a refusal (to forget or forsake — flowing elsewhere, otherwise, all ways).

as Geonpul woman and academic Dr. Aileen Moreton-Robinson puts it: "the omnipresence of Indigenous sovereignty ontologically disturbs patriarchal white sovereignty's possession and its originary violence", remaining long before and beyond its (re)naming, living in and through the "presence of Indigenous people and their land… haunting the house that Jack built, shaking its foundations."

       this labour of erasure and disavowal, the negligence and outsourced empathy of the professional — the concurrent maintenance and elaboration of settlement that comes with the violence of accumulation and extraction — is what settlers strain to do, no matter the spaces they claim or politics they profess. indeed they come (to stay) in all shapes and sizes, colours and classes, strained ceaselessly to stop movement wherever they move. moving frantically only to remain in the same place, the same places they've always known, what they can't let go of and what they can't let up, whether it's a sense of pride or a sense of self, a plot of land or the other kind of plot that holds us in the frenzied stasis of the status quo — just like anyone else, it's what settlers hold and what holds them that determines their state and status.

"if known by his actions and how he justifies them, [the settler] sees himself as holding dominion over the earth and its flora and fauna, as the anthropocentric normal, and as more developed, more human, more deserving than other groups or species."

ultimately, of course, the settler comes to settle, ceaselessly staying put, singular and sorted, steadily spreading the frontier and "making a new 'home'", write decolonial scholars Tuck and Yang, "that is rooted in a homesteading worldview where the wild land and wild people were made for his benefit."

in other words... 'but why are some of the worst cunts gay and melinated?' solid class analysis gets us closer to an answer, revealing some expansive array of arranged theft and deception, but eventually it can end up feeling like playing statistics mixed through with some vague appeal to an abstract and assumed humanity, like calculating the probability of a person turning up true off of some strange collection of assigned categories, the origins of which so often seem to remain unseen. seems easier to simply repeat the depraved illogics of modernity's granddaddys, pointed now in the opposite direction: the more white the less human, and the blacker the better, and if you find yourself out by the wayside of this impossible and expanding arithmetic or if you're ever brave enough to ask why we're all talking like this, then i guess you're just an anomaly, and that's just tooooooooo bad.

this seems to be the uncomfortable and comforting lie at the heart of (what often gets passed as) identity politics, a phrase that has been all but emptied of meaning through its disparate usages by straight up racists and so-called radicals. it doesn't seem to matter at all how any one of us identifies, beyond what this collectively reveals of the (im)material conditions that (re)produce these categories that we then seek to claim, which are still always contextual and localised and never totally overdetermined even in this global hellscape we sometimes mistake for reality.

of course, that global hellscape remains capitalist and white supremacist, patriarchal and colonial; a war with innumerable fronts appearing across and as these interlocking systems of category and control. as the Black feminists of the Combahee River Collective wrote in 1977: "the psychological toll of being a Black woman and the difficulties this presents in reaching political consciousness and doing political work can never be underestimated. [...] We are dispossessed psychologically and on every other level, and yet we feel the necessity to struggle to change the condition of all Black women. In A Black Feminist's Search for Sisterhood, Michele Wallace arrives at this conclusion: 'We exist as women who are Black who are feminists, each stranded for the moment, working independently because there is not yet an environment in this society remotely congenial to our struggle — because, being on the bottom, we would have to do what no one else has done: we would have to fight the world.'"

      this seems as true and clear as ever. it seems there remains something else here that connects us, something deeper to our difference that is (in the end and beginning) the same. many struggles one fight, the dream of communism, the recognition that Sovereignty Never Ceded and that this shit is killing you too however much more slowly and that "if Black women were free, it would mean that everyone else would have to be free since our freedom would necessitate the destruction of all the systems of oppression." Blackfella, whitefella, yellafella, anyfella.

caught in the peripheral so we kept turning, like a
beautiful ecology we find unity in diversity, sustenance
in sharing the sun, severing the self and staying on
the run to and for another home, migrants for only a
little while. all the land back remains the horizon, and
this is no metaphor. we're not free til we're all free. in
a situation of war, we forget and then remember that
every line is arbitrary. in heart and head.

so settler colonialism attempts to steal our memories,
histories and futures, so decolonisation is in part a
project of recognition and remembrance, so we hope
to remember and retell a story that found a way from
no way, to follow another feel that came and went
elsewhere, went wayward, struggling for a life together
where we remember all of this as a funny old story we
got bored of telling.

picking up the thing to drop it again,
something like the moon always
on the run again
cuz none of this is any one of ours
when it's for all of us.

weird poem death

i get a feeling you see me and feel at some level afraid

that last sentence is literal: it is a feeling

i think about my face and smile, laugh if applicable

i think about what is interacting when we interact

which layer of me do you see when our eyes meet
(and there again another metaphor of relation)

we talked in whispers when we still knew god

i remember being 6 years old on the steps of mount
carmel with the sun too bright the air too thick
stuck on some odyssey i woke up in the chant of
but back to the background i didn't yet know was there
in the refugee encampment of the enlightenment
another offering of abraham amid
piles of plenty and promise

what is poetry anyway

it's not getting any easier to believe in art as
emancipatory when i don't feel like an artist

a deterministic kind of governance occupies the half
of my brain i leave in the pickle jar while the rest
i leave up to divine intervention

(depression is the endless in between
sometimes a song or sometimes a sometimes
feeling of pain or blah
blah blah what happened to my brain i will find it
at the end of the ruler
measuring out lines on a weekly schedule
of mundane objectives ticked off like a
shopping list for an emotionally absent father
of three dickhead gilroy boys always telling
their shiftworker mother to get fucked
master chief on the screen looking on disappointed
but who would know)

it's sickening the way the planet was robbed of its
name and fed its own dirty laundry like a weird
do-it-yourself-in-the-microwave nightmare fetish

meanwhile i'm tired and sore but mostly okay, hehe
follow me

(the street is quiet sometimes and other
times i stay inside
i try when i can
to eat something or say something
to remember there's magic because
there has to be

because before i knew anything
about anything i made
magic on my keyboard
because now i collect
dust on my eyelids for a little joke
and a bit of warmth)

there's always a long way left to go
in the undercommons of the unaccountable
where it's way too late for poetry
when we've gone past the moon
in a spaceship made of squishy saphire
and silver shoestrings

(sometimes a ghost is seen in a cloud
it is time to go to sleep
tomorrow we will try again)

heard the calls with and from hearts, heavy

couldn't find the words so flew outside

threw this flesh

against/along/across

a hard and ancient wind

that spans the earth

spins the black ground, we walk together

sing, eat and joke together

in rest, still

indifferently running

through with whatever fucken weather

yeah, inherited all of it without any writing

hand-me-downs top-to-bottom, hands held up

like thunder without lightning

like the stars that hold us

held up like a long wait

heavy cos it's holy

cuz, that light don't get this deep

cuz, that light never help us sleep

cuz, that light went out before, see

listen so you don't have to be told

without the feeling, inside

that holds this shit together, cuz

don't tell me you don't know when you know

you told me

it's a long way we came without knowing

the words, so let's go

like imagine sitting on the bottom of the ocean

an impossibly heavy feeling on the chest and skull

still smiling cos there's life here and it's strange

and terrifyingly beautiful

a thick and sticky subterranean swarm

of wondering angels, warning in their songs

that are ours to not forget

ours in that they stick with us and to us and so

finding ourselves stuck there

which was always here, we stick together

strained to remember where we're from

and where we're going, an itinerant assault upon

the enlightened violence of stasis, the lies

they keep telling whenever they try

and say that any of this is settled

a violent and fragile illusion that

slips again and again and again

when we hear, speak and see

every sound that

was never

silence

seen

but i didn't really read it
streamed the entire history of this interaction
by accident decided i didn't need it

but i wasn't even at the screen
just had it open taking a shit for the livestream
look at all the people who wanna see

but i guess i didn't believe it
saw some other story saying it was someone else
so i sorta thought it was some assortment of another
discourse of sorts
or something
so i kept scrolling

but i had this dream and i have this memory
and i hear some things you're saying about me
seems like a lot of work to be perceived sometimes
i wish i could just leave

but i really did, and it hurt so much that i didn't bleed
i closed my eyes and still cry every time
i even made this meme

but i didn't really read it
that feed had me talking funny
so i had to delete it

we look after each other to remember what came before to look after, to see what remains, to feel (in) the wake

rested beneath a shadow through this mutual passing, we feel around to find our grounds, having never left

found in movement in refusal of stillness, a refusal to move when moved on, unsettled by this song that moves us in (the sounds of movement, the friction felt in the harmony of a riot, the television crackling a sweet eulogy for itself)

so is it excessive to remember the self, given (to) all this? the self in excess of the flesh, the self we are given (to), these (un)holy gifts of me n mine?

sure, consideration of the self is maybe always a move from division, an itinerant indulgence that looks out to go in — your business is your business and so mine is mine, which would maybe be fine if we weren't already here, always already caught together in this communal struggle we call home

we want to live, yes, so we seek survival and stability, preserving protest to cultivate common good; but the emergency is ongoing and every floor appears uncertain, so we proceed always at risk of extending that enclosure past the fence posts, out past the borders we don't remember building but strain ourselves to stay behind (even as something else entirely stays moving us, through and out the outside, under, around)

(cuz, look: we already got them surrounded, some prior emergence had us feeling with another sound, drawn to the intrusion with a loving reluctance — prayers thrown and felt with the wind, a knowing look on a new moon, a funny story we got bored of reciting)

then flesh hits concrete cold metal on the back, pressed so the pain is felt in the chest and stomach, beneath each shoulder blade and between the eyes, burnt insides of a broken gum bursting with red, blue, and black

yeah, no borders between me and the ground, between the clouds and us, even the smallest ant knows it is so life falls away to the outside and in this cycle we fall with it, together in splinters of the new
familiar like it always was

Reading List

Akuno, Kali, and Ajamu Nangwaya. "Build and Fight: The Program and Strategy of Cooperation Jackson." Jackson Rising: The Struggle for Economic Democracy and Black Self Determination in Jackson, Mississippi. Montreal, Québec: Daraja, 2017. 3-41.

Artist, American. "Black Gooey Universe." unbag - Issue 2: End. 2018.

Barta, Tony. "Relations of Genocide : Land and Lives in the Colonization of Australia." Genocide 2 (2008): 102-14.

Bellacasa, Maria Puig De La. "Matters of Care in Technoscience: Assembling Neglected Things." Social Studies of Science 41.1 (2010): 85-106.

Benjamin, Walter. "On the Concept of History." Frankfurt School: On the Concept of History by Walter Benjamin. Trans. Dennis Redmond. 2001[1940].

Chun, Wendy Hui Kyong. "Introduction: Race And/As Technology; Or, How To Do Things To Race." Camera Obscura: Feminism, Culture, and Media Studies 24.1 (2009): 7-35.

Coulthard, Glen Sean. Red Skin, White Masks: Rejecting the Colonial Politics of Recognition. Minneapolis: University of Minnesota, 2014.

Day, Iyko. "Being or Nothingness: Indigeneity, Antiblackness, and Settler Colonial Critique." Critical Ethnic Studies 1.2 (2015): 102.

Dean, Aria. "On The Black Generic." NGV. 2017.

Foucault, Michel. The Archaeology of Knowledge: Michel Foucault. Tavistock Publications, 1972.

Fraser, Nancy. "Rethinking the Public Sphere: A Contribution to the Critique of Actually Existing Democracy." Social Text 25/26 (1990): 56.

Galloway, Alexander R. "The Black Box Of The World." Cultureandcommunication.org. 2018.

Goodall, Heather. Invasion to Embassy: Land in Aboriginal Politics in New South Wales, 1770-1972. Sydney: Sydney University Press, 2008.

Haber, Benjamin. "The Queer Ontology of Digital Method." WSQ: Womens Studies Quarterly 44.3-4 (2016): 150-69.

Hall, Stuart. "The West and the Rest: Discourse and Power." Race and Racialization, 2E: Essential Readings. 2nd ed. Canadian Scholars, 2018. 85-95.

Haraway, Donna Jeanne. A Cyborg Manifesto: Science, Technology, and Socialist-feminism in the Late Twentieth Century. 2009.

Harney, Stefano, and Fred Moten. The Undercommons: Fugitive Planning & Black Study. Wivenhoe: Minor Compositions, 2013.

Hartman, Saidiya V. Scenes of Subjection: Terror, Slavery, and Self-making in Nineteenth-century America. New York: Oxford University Press, 2010.

Hartman, Saidiya V., and Frank B. Wilderson. "The Position of the Unthought." Qui Parle 13.2 (2003).

Harvey, David. "The 'New' Imperialism: Accumulation by Dispossession." Socialist Register 40 (2009).

Horne, Gerald. "The Apocalypse Of Settler Colonialism." Monthly Review. 2018.

Keeling, Kara. The Witch's Flight: The Cinematic, the Black Femme, and the Image of Common Sense. Durham: Duke University Press, 2007.

Marx, Karl. "Capital: A Critique of Political Economy | Volume 1." Marxists Internet Archive. 2015[1867].

Mignolo, Walter. Local Histories/global Designs: Coloniality, Subaltern Knowledges, and Border Thinking. Princeton, NJ: Princeton University Press, 2012.

Moreton-Robinson, Aileen. The White Possessive: Property, Power, and Indigenous Sovereignty. Minneapolis: University of Minnesota, 2015.

Moten, Fred. "Blackness and Poetry." Evening Will Come 55 (2015). The Volta.

Moten, Fred. "Consent Not to Be a Single Being." Stolen Life. Durham: Duke University Press, 2018.

Nakata, Martin. "The Cultural Interface." The Australian Journal of Indigenous Education 36 (2007): 7-14.

Pascoe, Bruce. Dark Emu, Black Seeds: Agriculture or Accident? Broome: Magabala, 2016.

Robinson, Cedric J. Black Marxism: The Making of the Black Radical Tradition. 2nd ed. Chapel Hill and London: University of North Carolina, 2000.

Rose, Deborah Bird. "Climate Change and the Question of Community." Deborah Bird Rose | Love at the Edge of Extinction. 2014.

Said, Edward W. Orientalism. Routledge & Kegen Paul, 1978.

Sexton, Jared. "The Social Life of Social Death: On Afro-Pessimism and Black Optimism." InTensions 5 (2011). York University.

Silver, Lynette Ramsay. The Battle of Vinegar Hill: Australia's Irish Rebellion. Sydney: Doubleday, 1989.

Smith, Linda Tuhiwai. Decolonizing Methodologies: Research and Indigenous Peoples. 2nd ed. Zed, 2012.

Spillers, Hortense. "The Idea Of Black Culture." University of Waterloo English Department. 2013.

Spivak, Gayatri Chakravorty. "Critical Intimacy: An Interview with Gayatri Chakravorty Spivak." Interview by Steve Paulson. Las Angeles Review of Books. 2016.

Tuck, Eve and K. Wayne Yang. "Decolonization is Not a Metaphor." Decolonization: Indigeneity, Education & Society 1.1 (2012):1-40.

Weeks, Kathi. The Problem with Work: Feminism, Marxism, Antiwork Politics, and Postwork Imaginaries. Durham: Duke University Press, 2011.

Wilderson, Frank, III. "Gramsci's Black Marx: Whither the Slave in Civil Society?" Social Identities 9.2 (2003): 225-40.

Wolfe, Patrick. "Settler Colonialism and the Elimination of the Native." Journal of Genocide Research 8.4 (2006): 387-409.

Wu, Danielle. "Do Androids Dream of Whiteness?" unbag - Issue 3: Reverie. 2018.

Wynter, Sylvia. "Unsettling The Coloniality Of Being/Power/Truth/Freedom: Towards The Human, After Man, Its Overrepresentation—An Argument." CR: The New Centennial Review 3.3 (2003): 257-337.

One Extra Large Coffin For My Luxury SUV Please

cool steel apple magic keyboard of crystal off-white
phlegm glued to a hundred fat hairy fingers
attached to a much larger object, its colour indecipherable

i walk outside and water the strawberries, taking care
to avoid the daddy long legs hiding beneath
the tap
the water splashes on my toes
and i exhale

inside the tv mumbles murder and mischief
mark ferguson ushering in the apocalypse with cool
indifference
an ocean frozen over in his pupils

moons come and go and the hairs on my face turn
yellow and green like scotch thistles spiralling
up the grand internal staircase of my luxury private
library in my masterton display home made of gold
bricks and black marble
towering over the hills like a jumbotron
headstone

fred moten via denise ferreira de silva and
innumerable others reminds us of the dangers
of 'democratising sovereignty'
"when people start thinking of their house
as their castle, that's bad"
i nod at my desk at my computer i paid for
with my money i earned from my job

i go to work and pray on the tl
to preserve this queer disturbance, cloaked
and stirred into the not so subtle sounds and smells
of our thick and broken skin and hair
melting, beautiful and bronze beneath the feet
of a thousand steel-capped boots, wide awake
in hi-vis, the sun shining down on another
year in paradise

we come full circle
broken futures never promised the truth
funny stories we told our daughters
a false wholeness rain, a red sun, the roots
running to a place we'd always been finding a home where we left it
empty like an asteroid belt massive, powerful and terrifying like love, and life
lived in between spaces the movements
of things
any path gets us there we didn't say we already knew

ACKNOWLEDGEMENTS

Thanks Dan & Subbed In for bringing this book to life.

Thanks Trish for the seriously good cover art.

Thanks Sniz & Mani & Mum & Dad & Aunty &
all the friends in and of the undercommons, the
underground commoners
and all our kin.

This is for and from all of us.

<3

ABOUT THE AUTHOR

kenji kinz is barely pseudonymous for not a writer
who still sleeps on Dharug land, 2148.

ABOUT SUBBED IN

Subbed In is an independent literarararararararary organisation and (very) small publisher. Subbed In programs events and publishes award-winning books that aim to elevate the voices of trans people, people of colour, non-binary people, sex workers, women, people with a disability, LGBTQIA+ people, First Nations people, survivors, working class people, and anyone who finds themselves on the margins of the supremely white, cis, heteronormative, capitalist, colonial, ableist, patriarchal hellscape in which we live. We jam econo.

www.subbed.in

ALSO AVAILABLE FROM SUBBED IN

In The Drink
by Emily Crocker

Sexy Tales of Paleontology
by Patrick Lenton

*When I die slingshot my ashes
onto the surface of the moon*
by Jennifer Nguyen

blur by the
by Cham Zhi Yi

HAUNT (THE KOOLIE)
by Jason Gray

The Hostage
by Šime Knežević

*If you're sexy and you know
it slap your hams*
by Eloise Grills

wheeze
by Marcus Whale

Parenthetical Bodies
by Alex Gallagher

The Naming
by Aisyah Shah Idil

Girls and Buoyant
by Emily Crocker

Uncle Hercules and other lies
by Patrick Lenton

www.subbed.in

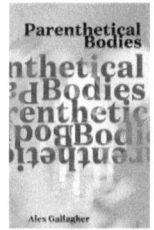

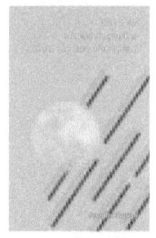

www.ingramcontent.com/pod-product-compliance
Lightning Source LLC
Chambersburg PA
CBHW022021290426
44109CB00015B/1255